MULLIGANS

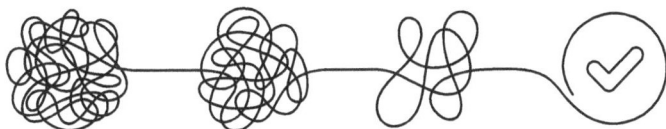

**RECOVERY
THOUGHTS FOR
THOSE IN DESPERATE
NEED OF A "DO-OVER"**

Mul·li·gan: a free shot sometimes given in informal golf when the previous shot was poorly played.

(Synonyms include re-do, freebee, and do-over)

LOGAN BRADFORD SAUNDERS

dustjacket

Published by Dust Jacket Press

Mulligans, Recovery Thoughts for Those in Desperate Need of a "Do-Over" / Logan Bradford Saunders

ISBN: 978-1-953285-77-5

Dust Jacket Press
P.O. Box 721243
Oklahoma City, OK 73172
www.dustjacket.com

All Scripture quotations not otherwise designated are from the King James Version of the Bible.

PUBLISHER'S NOTE: All bold formatting of words and phrases within Scripture quotations throughout this book has been added by the author for emphasis and does not appear in the Scripture quotations themselves.

Cover and interior design by D.E. West - www.zaqdesigns.com
with Dust Jacket Press Creative Services

Printed in the United States of America

dustjacket

DEDICATION

To my wife, Elsie

◇ ◇ ◇

Thank you for fighting for me.

You.

Me.

And a cup of coffee.

—Logan

◇ ◇ ◇

C O N T E N T S

Introduction vii

1. Broken Jar 1
2. All Things...5
3. Thank You, Kindly 9
4. Worried To Death 13
5. Paddle Boat 17
6. Is This Thing On?....................................21
7. Iron Sharpens Iron 25
8. That's a Fair Trade 29
9. Party of Two 33
10. Mad As Hell 37
11. Apples and Oranges 41
12. Check Engine Light..................................45
13. Half-Baked..49
14. I'm Not Sick 53
15. How Are You? 57
16. New Hope 61

17. Two Boats and a Helicopter 65

18. Checkmate 69

19. Not Today Satan 73

20. Totaled 77

21. IDK 81

23. Sun Stand Still 89

24. Through The Roof 93

25. Lost & Found 97

26. Who Told You That? 101

27. You Seem Different 105

28. You Complete Me? 109

29. Just an Ass 113

30. Lamp 117

31. Failing Up 121

About the Author 125

◇ ◇ ◇

INTRODUCTION

After years of abusing alcohol, my life was in a very deep valley. My wife had separated from me, my family had some pretty deep wounds, and I couldn't keep a job to save my life. I sat alone in my house, piss drunk, and filled with regret. I prayed to God for a mulligan. I thought if I had one more "second" chance, I would do everything differently.

Then I heard a knock on the front door. My wife stood there in what used to be "our" entry way and told me if I went to Good Landing Recovery, we could still have a chance at redemption.

The following months were equal parts war and revival. I cried. I praised. I was angry. I was grateful. I was depressed. I was inspired. I was empty. I was whole.

God had grabbed me by the hand (and sometimes the collar) and showed me that nothing was too broken to fix. He had no problem showing me just what kind of God he is. One of hope. Conviction. Love. Healing. Understanding.

And I'm very thankful to say, He is also a God of mulligans.

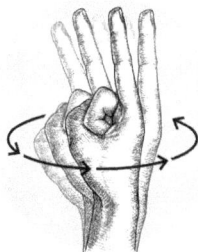

◇ ◇ ◇

1

BROKEN JAR

In the late 15th century, the emperor of China had a collection of precious jars and bowls that were chipped, cracked, or completely broken. I'm not sure if these items had a lot of sentimental or historical value, but he demanded that his craftsmen find a way to restore them back to their former beauty. After a lot of thought, the craftsmen had a stroke of genius: they filled the cracks with gold. This process is called "Kintsugi". It is rumored that the emperor was so pleased with the improved pottery, he started breaking jars on purpose. The broken pottery went from worthless to priceless because it had been repaired with gold.

David wrote in **Psalm 31:12**,
*"I have been forgotten like one who is dead.
I have become like a broken vessel."*

He continues to say later in **Psalm 147:3,**
*"He heals the broken hearted
and binds up their wounds."*

I spent the first half of my recovery thinking it would be good enough to just "get back to the old me". I thought that would give me enough self-worth and my family enough peace of mind. I had no idea, however, that God had much bigger plans for my recovery and for my life. It is so easy to settle when you have been in a challenging season, and I was selling myself (and God) short.

Why should I settle for "the old me", when God can pick up my pieces, fill my brokenness with his Holy Spirit, and put me back together as something so much more valuable than before?

Have you been saying the same things I did? Do you have some pretty big cracks in your heart and life?
Well, breathe easy…

Our Heavenly Father knows just what to do with a broken jar.

_____

_____

_____

_____

_____

_____

MULLIGANS

◇ ◇ ◇

2

ALL THINGS

One of the biggest lies we were told growing up was that the most important thing someone can do is be "goal" oriented. So, on my second day in rehab I set my goals. I wanted my life back, right? All at once and right now.

> I wanted to stop hating myself.
> I wanted my marriage to be fruitful.
> I wanted my family to trust me again.
> I wanted to make money.

However, the founder of Good Landing Recovery, Trey Lewis delivered a message one Friday night that completely changed my way of thinking. Trey said, "This probably isn't your sexiest season…where you show up at the cookout with a new car and all of the money in your bank account. This is a season where you have to focus on you and God and that's IT. And it's gonna take this season, to get to that season."

Trey helped me realize, that if I really did want all those things, I needed to be "growth" oriented instead of "goal" oriented. My next step had to be to shut up, sit down, and grow. So, I soaked up all the wisdom I could. I took notes. I read everything in front of me. I did just what Trey said…I focused on God and myself. And I grew.

After a while, the most interesting thing started to happen. All those goals I had before—the marriage, the family, the money, and even loving myself—they didn't move closer to me, I moved closer to them. Today, all of those goals I wanted have come true, because I grew.

It's true what is said in **Matthew 6:33**,
"But seek first the kingdom of God, and
all things *will be added to you."*

It's okay to not be in your season of winning yet. If you are growing that means that something is coming. So, relax and grow first. Keep yourself watered with wisdom and fertilized with faith…and God will show you more fruit than you ever imagined.

_____

_____

_____

_____

_____

MULLIGANS

◇ ◇ ◇

3
THANK YOU, KINDLY

I have given so many halfhearted "I'm sorrys" it's embarrassing. It got to the point where I didn't even know if I truly meant the apology I was giving. All my mistakes followed me around like a cartoon cloud and the weight of them would sometimes be unbearable.

But as I grew and sobriety began to be a reality instead of a hope, I realized one of the most powerful principles in my recovery: there is more power in "Thank you" than "I'm sorry".

Saying your millionth apology doesn't really do anything for yourself or the other person. I mean, how much weight does an apology we give really have anymore? Gratitude, however, lifts them up. It gives them validation and shows them that you are growing. It also brings you a sense of peace that apologies simply cannot give you.

So, instead of saying, "I'm sorry for everything", I started saying, "Thank you for being there through everything." Instead of saying, "I'm sorry for not show-ing up", I said, "Thank you for showing up."

If that principle applies to our earthly relationships, doesn't it ring even more true to our Heavenly Father? The Father that can see through the fake apologies and those empty "This is the last time(s)."

1 Chronicles 16:34
"Give thanks to the Lord, for he is good;
his love endures forever."

There may be a time to say, "forgive me" to those you've let down, but start instead with gratitude. If you can't find the words to say to God or your loved ones, just remember:

There is more power in
"Thank you" than "I'm sorry".

_____

_____

_____

_____

_____

_____

_____

MULLIGANS

◇ ◇ ◇

4

WORRIED TO DEATH

Anxiety and worry have been close "friends" of mine for a while now. I've literally been bed ridden due to countless "what ifs?" and unrealistic hypotheticals time and time again. Unfortunately, it took rock bottom for me to understand that worry, like any other tactic used by the devil, can be defeated.

I am grateful for Louie Giglio's book, *Winning The War on Worry*. (This book changed my life. I am plugging it. Go buy it.) Louie said, "Worship and worry cannot occupy the same space; they can't both fill our mouths at the same time. One always displaces the other."

I know what you're thinking because I was thinking the same thing-*there is no possible way that praise alone can defeat all my worries*. I am here to tell you that I was dead wrong, and it can. Worry is powerless over worship. It's incredible.

Psalms 34:1-3
"I bless God every chance I get; my lungs expand with his praise. I live and breathe God; if things aren't

*going well, hear this and be happy: Join me in
spreading the news; together let's get the word
out. God met me more than halfway,
he freed me from my anxious fears."*

Why are we so inclined to hold onto our worries like a child holds onto a stuffed animal? Maybe our worries have been a crutch or excuse for our behavior? Maybe we just get used to being worried and it seems, "normal"? Can I tell you something…Jesus wants to give us a new normal; one free of worry, because he cares for us.

So, to change your worried focus to a worship focus…

- Use praise and worship to focus on God.
- Use gratitude to focus on the good things of God.
- Use kindness to others to serve God.

Whatever form of praise you can think of, do it. It works. Because, worship and worry cannot occupy the same space.

_____

_____

_____

MULLIGANS

_____

_____

_____

_____

_____

_____

_____

_____

_____

_____

_____

_____

_____

_____

_____

_____

_____

_____

_____

_____

_____

◇ ◇ ◇

5

PADDLE BOAT

I am blessed to say that I have a great Dad. When my brother and I turned 15, he took us on our own little trips to teach us what it means to be a man. We discussed many things: how a man should lead his family, our walk with God, and sexual impurity. The good. The awkward. All of it.

My brother Landon's trip was a little bit more dramatic than mine.

Though he was feeling a little under the weather, the trip was promised to Landon and Dad intended to keep his word. The lake house they borrowed for this occasion came equipped with a paddle boat that was ideal for meaningful conversations. After some good talks "at sea" they brought the paddle boat back into the dock and headed up the hill for dinner. After the sun went down, they looked out and saw a problem: the borrowed paddle boat had come untied from the dock and was floating in the middle of the lake!

My Dad thought, "What a great teaching moment about taking responsibility". Dad explained to Landon that they had to retrieve the boat since they had borrowed it. While Dad weighed their options, Landon begged to swim out to the boat and get it. With few options that could work, Dad grudgingly agreed, though he said he was going to swim with Landon.

My brother stripped down to his boxers, dove in, and swam like an Olympic swimmer. Dad however, was distracted with Landon's safety, and did not carefully weigh the effects of sickness, the meal they had just eaten, or all the clothes he elected to keep on when he jumped in. While Landon was almost to the paddle boat, Dad struggled almost immediately. As he became aware of the gravity of his situation, Dad commanded Landon to get to the boat where he'd be safe. Looking back at the dock and then over to the boat, dad realized both were too far out of reach.

Panic struck his body. His head bobbed above and below the water. In the distance he faintly saw other lake houses with their lights on and began to scream. "Help! Please!". His head went back under the water. A final kick of his feet got him just high enough for another shout… "Help! Please! Someone!"

At this point he starts praying to the Lord to save him from this tragedy. He thought about what it would do to my brother and it broke his heart.

His head bobbed above the water one last time and he took what he believed to be his final breath. Then my father began to sink. One hand raised above the water—that's all that was left of my Dad's life. It was quiet.

* Slap!*

A hand grabs onto my Dad and swims him all the way to shore. Dad was stunned to see Landon. My brother ignored my dad's request to stay on the paddle boat and he saved my father's life that day.

Psalm 116:8
"For you have rescued my soul from death,
My eyes from tears, and my feet from stumbling."

You see, I've felt like my Dad for most of my adult life, with my head bobbing in and out of the water, so close to drowning. My past was too far gone to fix, and my future was out of reach and impossible. But God saw my hand raised just above the water line. He came to where I was, lifted me up, and swam me to shore. God sees your hand too. All you need to do is raise it. All you need to do is submit to God's plan to save you and rescue you. I am so glad I placed my hand in God's hand.

LOGAN BRADFORD SAUNDERS

◇ ◇ ◇

6

IS THIS THING ON?

Prayer was a tough one for me to figure out. I spent 29 years sending out prayers into the atmosphere, and what came back? Radio silence. I had felt his presence through worship. I had seen him work miracles in other people. But I couldn't get *the guy* on the phone to save my life! I thought of every possible reason why God wasn't responding to me:

> *I'm praying the wrong prayers.*
> *My prayers are too small.*
> *My prayers are too big.*
> *My sins are too great.*

The list goes on and on.

Looking back now though, the answer is pretty simple.

I was in a place emotionally to send out prayers, but I wasn't in a place spiritually to receive responses. My transmitter was on, but I forgot to turn on my receiver. Then I got mad at the Lord for ghosting me!

I guess I missed what David wrote in **Psalm 22:24**
"For he did not despise or abhor the afflicted;
he did not hide his face from me,
but heard when I cried to him."

God wasn't ghosting me, he was hearing me. I, however, was unwilling to hear him; and until I humbled myself, my receiver would remain forever in the "off" position.

Also, changing the way I prayed unlocked a new type of exchange that I never saw coming. I began starting my prayers with "Hey God". I know that sounds a little silly, but that simple change transformed what felt like a transaction between co-workers, into a conversation between friends.

I can talk to my friends all day long. But I also make sure I'm in a place to listen when they speak to me.

If you're having trouble getting answers from the Lord, check your connection. Are you really in a place spiritually to hear His voice? God is your friend…and he's waiting to have a conversation.

_____

_____

_____

MULLIGANS

_____

_____

_____

_____

_____

_____

_____

_____

_____

_____

_____

_____

_____

_____

_____

_____

_____

_____

_____

_____

◇ ◇ ◇

7

IRON SHARPENS IRON

Whether it be in a church group, recovery meeting, or whatever your next season is, you are going to see people going about recovery totally the wrong way. It could be simply not taking it seriously. It could be putting themselves in high-risk situations. It could even be actively using and trying to be slick about it. (We, as addicts, are terrific liars…until we aren't.)

I've seen it all.

This may be a harsh truth but it is still a truth: there are *winners* and *losers* in recovery.

So, what do you do when you're playing such a high risk, life or death game? I think the answer is pretty easy actually: Surround yourself with other winners who constantly challenge you to be better. For instance, before I started my recovery journey, the last book I read was *Holes* in the 5th grade. Yes, I'm in my thirties; and yes, this is embarrassing. But at Good Landing I met my friend, Marlon. Marlon is a winner. He always asked me what book I was reading and talked to me about other books I should get into. Marlon and I grew together because we had the same goal for recovery and the same heart for the Lord. Marlon is my buddy.

1 Corinthians 15:33
"If we want to know the Lord and become more like him, we must surround ourselves with friends who desire the same things. If we don't, we will desire the things of the world that inevitably lead to ruin."

If iron really does sharpen iron, I'm making sure the people on my team are sharp as knives, carving me into the man God destined me to be.

How sharp are the people around you? How sharp are the knives that you surround yourself with? Are they making you sharper with conviction or dull with complacency?

_____

_____

_____

_____

_____

_____

_____

MULLIGANS

◇ ◇ ◇

MULLIGANS

8

THAT'S A FAIR TRADE

I think it's safe to say that no one is 100% excited to get sober. To me, giving up alcohol meant boring New Year's Eves, quiet birthdays, and having water at fancy restaurants instead of my beloved French reds. In a lot of ways, I felt weaker for trading in beer for La Croix; but like many things, time and space gave me some much needed perspective. I didn't realize all I would gain from surrender.

Here's a good exercise I use to remind myself when the going gets tough in my sobriety:

- I'm trading a wild birthday party for a vacation with my wife.
- I'm trading a cold beer during football season for financial security.
- I'm trading New Year's Eve for Christmas morning with my kids.
- I'm trading things of the world, for my soul.

The list is constantly growing.

I never really took it literally what is said in **Matthew 16:26**

> *"And what do you benefit if you gain the whole world but lose your own soul? Is anything worth more than your soul?"*

The more I sit and reflect on everything sobriety has GIVEN me, the more I realize just how rich my life is becoming. And I'd trade a nickel of fun for a wealth of love any day of the week.

What trades are you making to get sober? How are you leveling up your life? What are you gaining? Is it a fair trade? It's more than fair. You are trading death for life!

_____

_____

_____

_____

_____

_____

_____

_____

_____

_____

MULLIGANS

◇ ◇ ◇

9

PARTY OF TWO

Spending one on one time with God has always been an awkward ordeal for me. Having a blind date with the Almighty, who already knows all of my failures is a little nerve racking to say the least. But, as I dissect why being alone with God makes me so uneasy, I've come to realize it all comes back to shame.

I'm uncomfortable about my shortcomings with alcohol (and a million other things), so I try and hide my face from the Lord. I used to hide myself in the crowd, bury myself in busyness, or distract myself with entertainment so I could avoid alone time all together. That is the opposite of what God wants from us and for us.

We need to understand that spending one on one time with the Lord isn't a shameful meeting, but a gathering filled with joy. His love for us is absolutely overwhelming, and he is desperate for a chance to teach us, encourage us, and make us feel loved.

Paul wrote in **Romans 8:38-39**
*"I'm absolutely convinced that nothing -
nothing living or dead, angelic or demonic, today
or tomorrow, high or low, thinkable or unthinkable -
absolutely nothing can get between us and
God's love because of the way that Jesus our
Master has embraced us."*

You see, alone time with God isn't an awkward dinner with a stranger; it's a meal with a Father whose love for you is immeasurable.

He will let you pick the place. The meal has already been paid for by the blood of Jesus Christ. And his eyes are going to light up when you walk into the room.

Your table is ready.

_____

_____

_____

_____

_____

_____

_____

MULLIGANS

◇ ◇ ◇

10

MAD AS HELL

There have been countless times where I have been frustrated in recovery and a few times where I've been flat out angry. Keeping my cool has been a constant challenge. Small things set me off, and if anything "big" happened it was a recipe for disaster. My body was screaming for alcohol, so it was not happy about it, and neither was I.

Luckily, I found **James 1:19-20**. It has saved me from allowing my negative emotions to spiral and provided me with the patience I needed in times of tension.

James wrote:

"My dear brothers and sisters, understand this:
Everyone should be quick to listen,
slow to speak, and slow to become angry."

Ever feel out of control emotionally? I know I have. I need this verse because, when I don't manage my emotions well, I create cracks in my life and relationships. It is part of the reason I drank; then drinking would only make the emotions and the fallout from them worse.

I know it's so much easier said than done, (especially the 'quick to listen' part) but I've found whatever message I'm trying to deliver lands more softly when I remember those words from James.

You see, people listen to the message when it is delivered softly, but they ignore the messenger when he shouts. Do you want to be heard or ignored?

So, remember:

> *Quick to listen.*
> *Slow to speak.*
> *Slow to become angry.*

◇ ◇ ◇

Prayer: *Lord, help me listen intently to others. Give me the patience to slow my words. And give me a heart that is slow to anger.*

_____

_____

_____

_____

_____

MULLIGANS

◇ ◇ ◇

11

APPLES AND ORANGES

Like pretty much everyone, I spent most of my teen-age years comparing myself to others. Based on my level of self-criticism, you'd think everyone I knew growing up was some sort of millionaire superhero. Maybe it's somewhat genetic, because when my older brother Landon was 10 years old, he came home from his first day of 5th grade very upset. We just moved school systems and he told our parents tearfully "I just feel like a molecule". (I know, heartbreaking sentiment. Impressive word usage.)

I can say without any doubt that I have never felt more like a molecule than I did in my first month of recovery.

I remember an especially painful night of "small-ness"; I made the mistake of scrolling on my phone. I saw many of my peers with their beautiful homes and families, and seemingly no problems at all. Here I was in rehab and with no guarantee of having any-thing when I recovered. Comparison was killing me!

The Lord helped me realize that though my story might look different from that of my peers, it was unique and offered something special: I could help many others fight what I was fighting. When I diverted my energy to helping serve others, the burden of self-comparison was lifted. Getting my eyes off myself and on to helping others was a gift.

That feeling of inadequacy was alleviated even more when I read **Jeremiah 29:11,**

> *"For I know the plans I have for you.*
> *Plans to prosper you and not to harm you.*
> *Plans to give you hope and a future."*

The enemy uses self-comparison as a tool to steal our hope, blind us of our trajectory, and silence our testimony. But God has a beautiful plan, and it is one that we should feel proud to be a part of. No failure is final, and God can use your past to create an amazing future!

_____

_____

_____

_____

_____

_____

_____

MULLIGANS

◇ ◇ ◇

12

CHECK ENGINE LIGHT

It's mid-July in Atlanta. It's noon. It's 99°F. The hood of my car is up and I'm standing on the side of I-85. I'm pretending that if I look hard enough at this engine, I'll somehow be equipped with the knowledge to fix whatever ails my smoking 2009 Pontiac G6.

Why was I sweating alongside the road, staring at a smoking car? Drinking had turned me into a procrastinator. My car's check engine light had been on since the day I got it, and I told myself I was "going to get my oil changed next paycheck". Every. Single. Paycheck.

God had turned on my internal check engine light time and time again, but I continually put off spiritual maintenance. When you put off solving problems, the costs always escalate. Now I was losing jobs, tearing holes in my family, and destroying my health. The warning lights were everywhere but nothing changed because I was always *going* to address the problem at hand, *next paycheck*.

I think the Lord was talking to me in **Jeremiah 7:13,**

"When I spoke to you persistently you did not listen, and when I called you, you did not answer."

Eventually, my life looked a lot like my car on that hot Atlanta interstate: broken down and in desperate need of repair. However, once I decided to address the warning signs the Lord was giving me, my life started to change for the better.

Emily Dickinson said, "If you take care of the little things, the big things will take care of themselves."

What are some of the little things the Lord is reminding you to take care of right now and not put off? Can you really wait until next paycheck? Is your spiritual check engine light on?

_____

_____

_____

_____

_____

_____

_____

_____

MULLIGANS

◇ ◇ ◇

13

HALF-BAKED

The second my detox was over, I screamed and cried to anyone who would listen, "I am ready!" I hadn't even started the rehab, mind you. Just the *detox*! I blindly believed I was ready to step back into the real world and face all the temptations awaiting me. I was so desperate for validation, that I was willing to risk it all, just to be able to say to a select few, "I am fine, see?" I even resented those who lovingly told me I needed "a little more time in the oven". Looking back, I am so grateful that I swallowed my pride and listened.

We are kind of like cake batter in the first stages of recovery. We probably taste "ok" as is, but with some time and warmth, we can turn into something beautiful. My battle with self-worth made me want to rush that process, rather than trusting it. When we do that, we not only sell ourselves short, but we rob our loved ones of the greatest version of ourselves. It took me a while to be okay with patiently trusting the process and just growing every day.

It all changed when I realized that recovery was something God had gifted me, something I should be proud of. That's an affirmation not a lot of people can say they have acquired. The validation I so desperately craved now came from God. He let me know that I was not only right where I needed to be but right WHEN I needed to be. I wasn't insecure about my position because I knew God put me there so he could complete the job he wanted to do within me.

Are you struggling with patience as you recover?

Isaiah 40:31 says,

> *"But they who wait for the LORD shall renew their strength; they shall mount up with wings like eagles; they shall run and not be weary; they shall walk and not faint."*

Are you looking for a shortcut instead of trusting the process? All my shortcuts led to short circuits. Let God do what he needs to do within you. Let him add all the ingredients, mix it all up, and throw in some heat. Don't settle for being half-baked.

_____

_____

_____

_____

MULLIGANS

◇ ◇ ◇

14

I'M NOT SICK

There are times in my life when people would ask if I was healthy. My answer was always, "yes, of course." I would often elaborate by saying, "I'm not sick now and I don't ever need to go to the doctor." I was sure I was a pretty healthy guy. Recently, however, I realized something: *just because I'm not sick does not mean I'm healthy.*

This being-sick-versus-being-healthy reality is true about every element of our lives, not just our physical bodies. So, just because my marriage doesn't require counseling, doesn't mean it's healthy. Just because friendships are "fine", doesn't mean they're healthy. And just because my relationship with God isn't sick, doesn't mean it's healthy.

Being sick is often about something that you did not choose, negatively affecting you. Being healthy, however, is about something good affecting you that you *did* choose. To be healthy is to choose to grow, learn, and change, every day.

You have seen sick trees and healthy trees…what's the difference? A sick tree has dead branches, a shrinking root system, and no fruit—it's one good storm from firewood. It has stopped growing. A healthy tree is strong, with green branches, an expanding root system, and full of fruit. It is growing and fruitful every day; and because of that it can handle the storms it will inevitably face.

I came to Christ at a young age. I knew God growing up because my dad was a pastor, and I went to church constantly. But my relationship with God was never healthy. I had accepted Christ, but I wasn't growing in my relationship with him. I was stagnant and eventually, life knocked me over.

Colossians 2:6-7 tells us,

"And now, just as you accepted Christ Jesus
as your Lord, you must continue to follow him.
Let your roots grow down into him, and let your lives
be built on him. Then your faith will grow strong
in the truth you were taught, and you will
overflow with thankfulness."

So just because our relationships, both earthly and heavenly, don't require medical attention, doesn't mean they are healthy. What can we do to keep them from being stagnant? How can we reinforce our roots? Make a decision to grow every day and you will be well on your way to a healthy life!

LOGAN BRADFORD SAUNDERS

◇ ◇ ◇

15

HOW ARE YOU?

I really do believe that mankind is naturally good overall. I think for the most part, when people come to me and say, "I'm a good person, I've just made some mistakes", they are telling me (and themselves) the truth. But let's stop talking about "who" we are for a bit and talk about "how" we are, every day.

Hebrews 13:8
*"Jesus Christ is the same, yesterday,
today, and forever more."*

This passage addresses one of the biggest differences between Jesus and mankind: consistency. John Maxwell wrote "We overestimate intensity and underestimate consistency." We must remember that who we are in a moment does not tell our story nearly as much as what we do every day.

- How many times have we said, "I just want to be more like Jesus", yet our emotions take over and we act more like the devil?

- How often have we wanted to be close to God, only to wander away the first chance we get?

- How many times have we wanted to show everyone a different person, only to make the same mistakes we have always made?

How do we change? We must remember, what we do or don't do *daily* determines if we develop or decline. If we truly want to be more like Jesus Christ, we must act like him *consistently*. And how do we do that? By growing in him, one day at a time, until it becomes a reflex. You see, **repetition** produces **reflex**. As I grow in Him every day I become more like Him, every day.

And before you know it, when someone cuts us off in traffic, gets in our face, or really disappoints us, our reflex won't be some unhinged reaction; our reflex will be to respond like Jesus. Because that's what we do consistently.

And that's how we are. Yesterday. Today. And forever more.

_____

_____

_____

_____

MULLIGANS

◇ ◇ ◇

16

NEW HOPE

When I look back at it, I was basically lost for most of my early adult life, I just didn't know it. I spent many years searching for fulfillment through work, through relationships, and eventually through drinking. Now I realize, any "fulfillment" I did gain from these things was cheap and fleeting. It took being completely broken down and defeated for me to see how lost I was and to find any new hope.

1 Peter 5:10

"The God of all grace, who called you to his
eternal glory in Christ, after you have suffered
a little while, will himself restore you and
make you strong, firm, and steadfast."

In my darkest hour, God helped my find my purpose, and my recovery would've have been virtually impossible without it. In fact, I believe finding your purpose is critical to recovery. To find my purpose, I had to first realize that I was a child of God, and God was the only one to whom I had to answer. After that,

I had to pray for God to guide me to discover my purpose. Finally, I had to ask myself some pretty tough questions:

- When do I feel the most fulfilled?
- What could I do that gives me the most joy?
- Does this bring the Lord more glory?
- Am I good at it?
- Can I do it anywhere for the rest of my life?

Here's what I have discovered about my purpose after a lot of prayer. I'm sure it will go through a few edits as the years pass but for now here is why I am here:

My purpose is…

> …*to lift up those who have fallen, quench their thirst for a better life with the water of hope, and show them that the Lord has bigger plans for them than they can even imagine.*

Once, I realized this purpose, it's almost like I started seeing the world in color for the first time. The sense of dread I had about my life was replaced with hope. I had a new mission, that I could do from anywhere, at any time. Best of all, this mission was one the Lord had assigned me…I was made for it and therefore that I could do it well.

So, if you're tired of wandering around aimlessly, it might be time to consider your God-given purpose. If you have not asked God to change your life, start there. Then ask yourself those same tough questions I asked. If you're anything like me, gaining that kind of clarity will change your life forever.

LOGAN BRADFORD SAUNDERS

◇ ◇ ◇

17

TWO BOATS AND A HELICOPTER

A massive hurricane approached a coastal town and the rain quickly turned to flooding. The reverend of the town fell to his knees on the church's front porch, as the water line rose around him. A neighbor in an SUV encouraged the pastor to come with him, but the pastor said, "No, God will save me." Then members of his congregation paddled over in a canoe, saying "Preacher! Come with us! The whole town is flooded!". He looked up to the sky and said, "No. I have faith in the Lord. He will save me."

The rising waters pushed the pastor up onto the balcony where he was spotted by someone on a fishing boat. The fisherman shouted, "Come on pastor, the levee is about to break! We must get out of here!" The reverend did not waver and responded over the thunder, "I shall remain! The Lord will see to it that I am safe!"

Finally, the reverend was forced to climb to the steeple of the church, his arms and legs wrapped around the cross. The National Guard hovered above him in a helicopter and began to plead with him through a megaphone. "Grab the ladder, preacher. This is your last chance!"

The preacher clung to his decision. He inevitably drowned in the flood.

Later, in heaven, the reverend spoke to God. "Heavenly Father, I had unwavering faith in you. Why did you not deliver me?" God responded, "I sent you a SUV, two boats and a helicopter. What else do you want from me, man?"

This funny little story is a great reminder of how stubborn we are when it comes to God's guidance. One of the ways the Lord speaks to us, is through circumstances. The reverend in this story obviously didn't realize that God was using circumstance to guide him. Sometimes apparently, we think we know more than God. In truth, we are just foolish, making things difficult when God has a simple solution.

In **Psalm 25:4-5**, we read,

> *"Make me to know your ways, O Lord;*
> *teach me your paths. Lead me in your truth and*
> *teach me, for you are the God of my salvation;*
> *for you I wait all the day long."*

Shamefully, while in treatment, I prayed that God would heal me so I could "get out of here". In hindsight, I now see that by being there, he was healing me. And doing it his way would ensure that I never had to go through it again.

How many times has God sent you "lifeboats" or "helicopters"? Has God ever shouted through a megaphone, so desperate to help you, but you were sure you knew better? Isn't it time to listen and trust his voice?

LOGAN BRADFORD SAUNDERS

◇ ◇ ◇

18

CHECKMATE

In August of 1888, a painting hung in a well-respected minister's home in Richmond, Virginia. The painting depicts the final moments of a chess match between the devil and a young man. The devil is grinning from ear to ear, with a gloating expression that can only signify his imminent victory.

With his hand on his forehead and fear in his eyes, the young man looks completely distraught in the painting. I'd be a little distraught too if I was sitting across from the devil, with my soul at stake over the outcome of a game of chess. The painting depicts the moment the devil said the one word this young man, like any chess player, hates the most: checkmate.

Paul Morphy (the world chess champion at the time) was invited over for dinner at the reverend's home. He couldn't resist a chess painting, so he excused himself from the table and began to carefully study the artwork. Eventually, he turned to the reverend and said, "I think I can take the young man's game and win."

The host responded, "Why, impossible! Not even you, Mr. Morphy, can retrieve that game."

So, they set up a table and assembled the pieces just as they were in the painting. Morphy studied the board, moved some pieces out of danger, and won the match for the young man. The devil had lost the match and a soul because the champion had one more move, he couldn't see.

That painting hung on that wall for years. And everyone who admired it just assumed that the devil was the victor. I think we look at the cards we've been dealt and assume that our "game" is already lost. But it is so crucial to remember that our Champion always has one more move. It's a move that can revitalize our faith, rid us of addictions, heal our families, and steady our incomes. His final move will always defeat the enemy. Every single time.

2 Timothy 4:18 tells us,

"The Lord will rescue me from every evil attack
and will bring me safely to his heavenly kingdom.
To Him be the glory. Forever and ever. Amen."

_____

_____

_____

MULLIGANS

◇ ◇ ◇

19

NOT TODAY SATAN

I'm not sure if it's a pride thing but I hate admitting when I am clearly under attack by the devil. I've spent all these years breathing in anxiety and coughing out worry, only to justify it by saying, "I guess I'm just an anxious person". I'd have these triumphant mornings of healing and growth then something small would come and ruin my whole day. I'd go from feeling so strong to completely overcome with weakness.

Finally, I went to some of the friends that I really respect and said "I think the devil is trying to mess with me today." Hearing myself say that out loud changed everything. My adversary was finally out from the shadows of my scattered mind and I could see him clearly.

Now we had a fair fight. One that I could win, because I realized that I am not the problem, HE is. And he is after my morning.

- If he can have my morning,
  he can have my day.

- If he can have my day,
  he can have my week.

- If he can have my week,
  he can have my month.

- If he can have my month,
  he can have my year.

- If he can have my year,
  he can have my life.

1 Peter 5:8-9

*"Be alert and of sober mind. Your enemy,
the devil, prowls around like a roaring lion, looking
for someone to devour. Resist him, standing firm
in the faith, because you know that the family of
believers throughout the world is undergoing
the same kind of sufferings."*

Identify your enemy. See him for what he is. Say his name. Rebuke him. And cut out his tongue with the armor of God. He has no power here.

_____

_____

_____

_____

_____

_____

_____

MULLIGANS

◇ ◇ ◇

20

TOTALED

During the first semester of my freshman year of college, I let my roommate borrow my beloved Volkswagen. It wasn't that nice of a car, but to 18-year-old Logan, it might as well have been a BMW. I gave him the keys, hopped on the train, and before I even got to my stop, he called me to deliver some pretty heartbreaking news. Someone had crashed into the back of my car while he was stopped at a red light. In short, the car was destroyed, and it would cost more to fix than the car itself was worth.

They always say, "you should get sober for YOU". I've heard that time after time, all throughout my recovery. Initially, "doing it for me" was not an option. You see, in my eyes, I wasn't worth enough to try and redeem. I didn't "cost enough" to even try to fix...I was totaled. My wife, however, saw something within me; something even valuable. So, because she was worth it (and because she asked me) I finally decided to go to recovery.

As I healed and grew, my reasons for getting sober evolved into something much deeper than just making my wife happy…I started to see my worth. My vision for myself began to grow. I wanted to be a better man. I wanted to feel healthy again. I wanted my parents to be proud of me. And eventually it even evolved into wanting to help others on their own recovery journey. There is no wrong reason to get better and the reasons only multiply the more that you grow spiritually. All you must do is start.

Matthew 6:26

"Look at the birds of the air; they do not sow or reap or store away in barns, and yet your heavenly Father feeds them. Are you not much more valuable than they?"

God does not ask you to come to him only if you are worthy…everyone is invited to find peace and healing in him. And there is always a reason to start getting better. Just because you're a little damaged, doesn't mean you're totaled.

Question: Are you believing the lie that you are not worth saving? Are you willing to take a step of faith in God's direction? He will heal you. He loves you.

MULLIGANS

◇ ◇ ◇

21

IDK

It was fall of my sophomore year of high school and I was flying from a summer internship. I arrived at the Atlanta airport (the biggest airport on Earth, by the way); I stepped off the plane located on concourse E, a long way from where my parents were picking me up. Like any 16-year-old, I made sure to call them to let them know that I landed safe and was on my way to baggage claim. I was really excited to see them after a long summer.

After about 40 minutes, I got a phone call from my dad. *"Where are you?"* I could hear the concern in his voice.

"I'm almost there! It's a long walk!", I responded.

"You're walking all the way from your gate!? Why didn't you take the 5-minute train ride to baggage claim??"

"I don't know! I got scared! I didn't want to mess up, so I just followed the signs to baggage claim."

I had just turned a 5-minute train ride into a 2 mile and 40 minute walk, because I was paralyzed by indecision.

I'd like to say that my decision-making anxiety has gotten better as I've gotten older, but I would only be kidding myself. If anything, I'd say it's gotten worse, because the stakes have gotten higher. What is my next "life step"? Do I take the job? Should I move? What is my purpose? Who do I marry?

All these questions are ones that require God's guidance, because indecision clouds our judgement and paralyzes our actions. Thankfully, God is willing to guide us if we are willing to trust him.

Proverbs 3:5-6

"Trust in the Lord with all your heart and lean not onto your own understanding. In all your ways, acknowledge him and he will direct your path."

Growing up, my dad saw me struggle with making decisions and showed me a fool-proof way to filter all the noise that comes along with decision-making.

The 4 Ways God Speaks To Me:

1. His Word: God speaks specifically to the decision at hand through the Bible.

2. His Holy Spirit: God speaks to me personally and intangibly.

3. Wise Counsel: God speaks through people I trust and respect to guide me through this decision-making process.

4. Circumstances: God speaks through situations so clearly that it can't be ignored.

Running my decisions through this filter saves me from making poor or even life altering choices; it blesses me with "the right call" repeatedly. This plan saves me from MY will and puts my future back in God's hands where it belongs.

If you're having trouble pulling the trigger on a big decision or are tired of constantly saying "I don't know", run it through this program. If the answer is "yes" through all four filters, you can act knowing you're safe and sound in God's will.

_____

_____

_____

_____

_____

_____

_____

_____

_____

_____

_____

_____

_____

_____

_____

_____

_____

_____

_____

_____

_____

_____

_____

_____

_____

_____

◇ ◇ ◇

22

FRESH WATER

A long time ago, a group of Peruvian sailors were caught in a massive storm and forced to drop anchor until the storm subsided. When the skies cleared, they realized their ship had sustained too much damage and they were stranded somewhere off the coast of South America. For days they suffered from dehydration, praying for another storm to come with fresh rainwater; but the blue skies only mocked them.

Eventually another vessel saw their plight and changed course to come and rescue them. When the approaching boat was finally within earshot, the sailors screamed, "Water! We need fresh water!". The captain of the rescuing ship responded with great confusion, "Lower your buckets!".

"No, we need fresh water!", they responded. "Lower your buckets!", the captain repeated.

The stranded ship reluctantly lowered their buckets into the ocean and, to their surprise, up came fresh water.

The crew had no idea that they had been anchored at the mouth of the mighty Amazon River for days. Here, the powerful flow of the Amazon River turns an ocean into millions of gallons of fresh water. The shore was far enough away the sailors had no idea that their salvation was all around them...they were literally swimming in it.

Why are we often so unwilling to see what is right in front of us? We beg for a better life and complain about bad luck, with no thought that maybe there's an answer nearby. We've spent our whole lives dying of thirst. But God satisfies every thirst. Jesus told a woman at a well one time, *"Anyone who drinks this water will soon become thirsty again. But those who drink the water I give will never be thirsty again. It becomes a fresh, bubbling spring within them, giving them eternal life."* **John 4:13-14**

He has all the thirst-quenching water our souls need, and it is within our reach. Just like those sailors, all we have to do is just lower our buckets and drink it.

_____

_____

_____

_____

_____

MULLIGANS

◇ ◇ ◇

23

SUN STAND STILL

As a kid, I used to pray for things like superpowers, or 1 million dollars, or a beach house on the moon. The sky was the limit because, hey its God we're talking about, right?

My prayers have gotten more boring now-a-day though. I pray just to not be tired at work. I pray to make the same amount of money this month as I did last month. I pray that the salsa I just ate doesn't give me heartburn.

It seems like the bigger I got, the smaller God got and the less faith I had for him to come through for me on big prayers. Honestly, I didn't even want to pray for the big ones because they seemed so farfetched. Clearly Joshua didn't have that problem.

Joshua 10:13
"Sun stand still over Gibeon, and you,
moon over Aijalon.

So the sun stood still and the moon stopped until the nation avenged itself on its enemies."

Can you imagine having enough faith in God to pray a prayer that big? For the sun and moon to halt their rotation just because I asked seems crazy. It's so easy for us get distracted by how big our problems are, we forget how much bigger God is. And He doesn't just want us to stop there.

Matthew 7:7 says,
"Keep on asking, and you will receive what you ask for. Keep on seeking, and you will find. Keep on knocking, and the door will be opened to you."

Are you holding back from the 'big asks' because you don't feel worthy? What are some of those big prayers you won't let yourself pray?

_____

_____

_____

_____

_____

_____

_____

MULLIGANS

◇ ◇ ◇

24

THROUGH THE ROOF

Reluctant. That's probably the best word to describe my attitude towards recovery early on. My wife put me in her car around 9pm and we drove 30 minutes to Dacula, Georgia where the main residential campus of Good Landing Recovery was. Upon arriving we quickly realized we were in the wrong place. The detox center was an hour in the other direction.

This was my chance. I could go home and "try again tomorrow," but my wife wasn't having it. She said, "please do this for us". I turned to butter, and we made the long drive. The rest was history.

In **Mark 2**, Jesus was teaching at a packed house, filled with people who'd come to witness his miracles. They were even gathered in the yard and streets surrounding the house. When four friends heard of Jesus' arrival, they laid their paralyzed friend on a mat and carried him across town to the house. Immediately, they realized the front door was not an option due to the crowd and had to come up with a new strategy. They climbed up onto the roof, dug through the ceiling, and lowered the paralyzed man onto the living room floor. Jesus saw the man, touched him, and simply said *"Son, your sins are forgiven."* The man stood up, picked up his mat, and walked out of the house.

It took four friends not giving up to save that man's life.

It took my wife not giving up to save mine.

They saw what kind of shape we were in, picked us up, and dropped us through the roof at the feet of Jesus.

Who are the people in your life that are willing to go literally above and beyond for you? And do you have any friends that could use your extra mile?

_____

_____

_____

_____

_____

_____

_____

_____

MULLIGANS

_____

_____

_____

_____

_____

_____

_____

_____

_____

_____

_____

_____

_____

_____

_____

_____

_____

_____

_____

◇ ◇ ◇

25

LOST & FOUND

One of my most heart-breaking memories was watching my dad cry at the foot of my bed as I pretended to be passed out drunk. He prayed "God, when he was a little boy, you promised me that he would do great things. You promised God! Where is that man you promised me? Take this from him. Please God!" Sadly, I was just so lost at that moment.

Being lost reminds me of a story in **Luke 15:11-24,** of a father who had two sons. The younger son had a wild spirit and demanded his portion of his inheritance. Getting his money, he left, traveled the world, and "*squandered his wealth on wild living*". He ended up broke and starving, working as a servant feeding pigs. (It even says he envied the pigs because at least they had something to eat.)

After a while, the son realized that he would have to swallow his pride and return home to his father. He would tell him "*Father, I have sinned against heaven and against you. I am no longer worthy to be called your son;*

make me like one of your hired servants.' So, he got up and went to his father.

But while he was still a long way off, his father saw him and was filled with compassion for him; he ran to his son, threw his arms around him and kissed him.

The son said to him, 'Father, I have sinned against heaven and against you. I am no longer worthy to be called your son.'

But the father said to his servants, 'Quick! Bring the best robe and put it on him. Put a ring on his finger and sandals on his feet. Bring the fattened calf and kill it. Let's have a feast and celebrate. For this son of mine was dead and is alive again; he was lost and is found.' So, they began to celebrate."

I don't know about you, but I've felt like the prodigal son for a long time. I've felt like I wasted blessings that both my heavenly and earthly father have given to me. Foolishly I thought I had to be close to God for him to see me again, let alone accept me. I didn't realize that even though I was still "a long way off" God saw me and was running towards me, ready to wrap his arms around me again. Are you basically a prodigal son or daughter to your heavenly father right now? Just take one step in his direction! He will run the rest of the way to you!

MULLIGANS

◇ ◇ ◇

26

WHO TOLD YOU THAT?

A guy in his early thirties was having a conversation with his coworker. We'll call the guy "Jim" and the coworker "Todd".

Todd: "Hey buddy. Are you doing okay? You seem off today."

Jim: "Honestly man, I've been arguing with my wife all week. Then, last night we got into this really big fight. This morning, we didn't say anything to each other. I don't know but I'll probably just talk to her when I get home."

Todd: "Who told you that?"

Jim: "What? That it's okay to talk when I get home?"

Todd: "No. Who told you that you'll make it home."

Jim called his wife.

Ouch. I've let pride stand in the way of healing my whole life. Like Jim, pride has caused me to make, "I'll make it home" assumptions. It's so easy for us to forget how tomorrow isn't promised to us and just how precious our loved ones really are. I can't believe how often we are willing to risk our loved ones not knowing how deeply we love them.

In **Proverbs 27:1** we read,

*"Do not boast about tomorrow,
for you do not know what the day may bring."*

What important conversations are you saving for tomorrow? What "I love you's" are you holding hostage? And is your reason for doing so worth it? Don't let silence be the last thing you say to those you love.

_____

_____

_____

_____

_____

_____

_____

_____

_____

_____

MULLIGANS

◇ ◇ ◇

27

YOU SEEM DIFFERENT

"You seem different." I've been getting a lot of that lately. I can only assume that is a good thing considering where I've been. (Can I get an amen?) And as I look at myself in the mirror, of course I seem different. I am different.

I had a conversation with a buddy about working out recently; he told me "I don't feel like I'm doing enough. I'm working out hard every day, but I'm still not seeing results."

"What is your input like?" I asked him. "Are you killing yourself at the gym and eating like an 8-year-old at home?".

I wish I understood this principle way earlier in my recovery: What you consume directly affects the time it takes to see results. Your input decides your output.

I decided halfway through recovery, that I would only *consume* things that would grow me closer to God and turn me into that better version of myself that we talked about in "Broken Jar". I started reading books. All my music choices became worship music. I started listening to John Maxwell's leadership podcast every morning. I only participated in conversations that filled my cup. (That last one was a big one.) I developed an appetite for growth and now I can't consume enough. I'm always hungry.

1 Timothy 4:15 explains it beautifully,

> *"Practice these things, immerse yourself in them, so that all may see your progress."*

Of course I seem different. My input completely changed so my output completely changed. And honestly, it happened fast. If you're getting frustrated with not seeing results, just check your input. French lawyer Anthelme Brillat-Savarin said it best: "You are, what you eat."

_____

_____

_____

_____

_____

_____

_____

MULLIGANS

◇ ◇ ◇

28

YOU COMPLETE ME?

This one is gonna hurt to write.

I started my recovery journey for my wife. She was the only reason I even stepped foot inside of Good Landing Recovery. My love for her was all that kept me going for years and honestly, I felt like I would die without her.

As I grew in my faith, however, God made something very clear to me: If I wanted to grow closer to him, I would have to let her go for a little while.

That broke my heart.
I mourned.

I was at my absolute lowest point in life without the only light my world had seen in years. I knew though, that I wasn't in a place to love someone; let alone lead a marriage and family the way that God tells us to in His word.

In **Ephesians 5:25** it says,

*"Husbands love your wives like Christ
loved the church and gave himself up for her."*

God didn't design us to be "completed" by someone else's love and two halves don't make you whole.

I finally realized that God is what completes us. We
both had to be entirely whole and running after God
individually. Only then could our marriage be something truly fruitful and beautiful. So, we both drew
nearer to God and the funniest thing happened; when
we finally reconnected, we felt closer than ever. It's like
God picked us up on opposite sides of the planet and
placed us right next to each other.

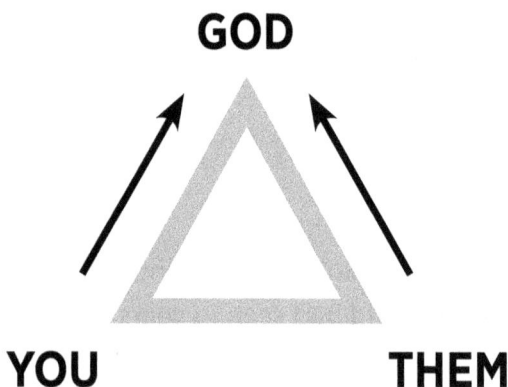

GOD

YOU   **THEM**

**The closer we move towards God,
the closer we get to each other.*

If you really love your spouse, boyfriend, or girl-friend you might have to let them go for a little while so you can heal and grow. Growing closer to God will make you the man or woman that they deserve. If you are both growing, the love that happens after that will be something better than either of you have ever experienced before.

_____

_____

_____

_____

_____

_____

_____

_____

_____

_____

_____

_____

_____

_____

_____

LOGAN BRADFORD SAUNDERS

◇ ◇ ◇

29

JUST AN ASS

When you have spent years with your self-worth at absolute zero, any praise can be just as addicting as the obstacle you just overcame. Therefore, when you win some confidence through recovery, you can become dangerously confident. You can think you've got this when you are still very much in a battle.

After a little bit of sober time, I've had a few opportunities to speak and share my story. (If you're into leading in any way you will too, trust me.) Don't get me wrong, I'm aware that there is a lot of power in my journey and what God has done in my life is an absolute miracle. But it's easy to get caught up in our "own" victories from time to time and be deluded into a false sense of security.

I am challenged by **I Corinthians 10:12**,

> *"If you think you are standing strong,*
> *be careful not to fall."*

When it comes to thinking too highly of ourselves, I love something John Maxwell said which I found both funny and convicting.

> It was the first Palm Sunday. Here came Jesus, riding into Jerusalem on a donkey. Great crowds began to shout "Hosanna! Hosanna!". Some threw down their coats on the road. Others spread out palm branches.

> The donkey perked up its ears. "Well," he said while swatting a fly off a mangy patch, "I had no idea they thought so highly of me!"

We get so wrapped up in our own performance and forget who the star of the show really is. We are not the star of the show, we're just the ass, Jesus rides on! It's so important that we remember God has conquered, is conquering, and will conquer all of our battles. He is doing it all. And "our" story is just a vessel to show people what kind of miracles his love can produce.

_____

_____

_____

_____

MULLIGANS

◇ ◇ ◇

30

LAMP

We've all probably heard **Psalm 119:105** somewhere over the course of our lives.

"Your word is a lamp unto my feet,
and a light unto my path."

I had to stop viewing that verse as something embroidered on one of my grandma's pillows and really analyze it to understand what it was trying to tell me.

Your word is a lamp.

Not a roaring bright flame. Not a spotlight. Not even a flashlight. A lamp.

Now, why would God give us something that shines so little? Wouldn't it be better if we could see more than just what is right in front of us? Why not give us enough light to see the whole landscape of what is to come?

I think there are two answers, and they are both simple:

1. We would see what His plans are for us and run in the other direction.

2. We would see what His plans are for us, and we would run ahead, inevitably messing the plan up with our good intentions.

Psalm 46:10
"Be still and know that I am God…"

It's just so human of us to want to rush the process. We want all the answers, in detail, and we want them all now. Of course, we say that God is in control, but we all still want one hand on the wheel! God knows if he gave us all the info, we would bail on a real relationship with him and just use him as a navigation app for our lives. But true intimacy with God happens when you don't need the whole picture laid out for you. True intimacy happens when you are grateful for the lamp.

_____

_____

_____

_____

MULLIGANS

◇ ◇ ◇

31

FAILING UP

Failure is a part of life. Mankind has been failing since the Garden of Eden and will continue to do so until Christ's return. I've heard many times after a relapse, "Now I have to completely start over". Their thought is that everything they'd done up to that point was "a waste of time" and all the good was erased due to their fall.

I too, had that same notion after two failed recovery attempts at different rehabs. I have discovered thankfully that this not the case, because the Lord can use "ALL things for his good". Here is what I have learned about failure and what I always remind myself when I fail in some way.

The Gifts of Failing

1. Failure Gives Me Perspective. (It helps me see the world around me more clearly.)

2. Failure Gives Me Humility. (It keeps me grounded and forces me to lean on God

because leaning on myself is no longer an option.)

3. Failure Gives Me Empathy. (It helps me understand situations through other people's hearts.)

4. Failure Gives Me Strategy. (Because I've failed, I know how to play the "game". That means I know what to look for and can change my game plan accordingly, this time, to win.)

David wrote in **Psalm 145:14,**

> *"He helps all those who are in trouble;*
> *he lifts those who have fallen."*

I think it's particularly important that we pay attention to who wrote that verse. David. The giant slayer. The King of Israel. The man after God's own heart. He was also David, the thief. The womanizer. The liar. The murderer.

If God can take David's many failures and turn them into something beautiful, why can't he pick us up, dust us off, and make us something new again too? I'm not saying that failing is something that has to happen, or that any of our shortcomings are a good thing; but

I am 100% certain that God can use them for good. Just like he did for David. Just like he did for me. And just like he can do for you.

_____

_____

_____

_____

_____

_____

_____

_____

_____

_____

_____

_____

_____

_____

_____

_____

_____

_____

_____

LOGAN BRADFORD SAUNDERS

_____

_____

_____

_____

_____

_____

_____

_____

_____

_____

_____

_____

_____

_____

_____

_____

_____

_____

_____

◇ ◇ ◇

ABOUT THE AUTHOR

My Dad was a pastor. I spent a lot of birthdays in church gymnasiums and was a pretty stereotypical "PK". I fell in love with God through worship music but honestly never had a real relationship with him until I was at absolute rock bottom. The worst part is, I was sure that what I had with God WAS real. I signed a record deal at 19, singing hooks for some relatively famous Atlanta rappers. The record deal went south and I ended up on both sides of the bar: as a bartender and bar patron. I tended bar for the better part of 10 years before I realized what alcohol had done to my life. My wonderful, Christ-loving, wife had about enough of me and frankly I don't blame her. I had about enough of me too. In one last act of grace, she brought me to my 3rd treatment center and God shook me back to life. That divine intervention catapulted me into a season of spiritual and mental growth. Since then, all I strive to do is save people just like me. One word at a time.

◇ ◇ ◇

www.ingramcontent.com/pod-product-compliance
Lightning Source LLC
Chambersburg PA
CBHW060327050426
42449CB00011B/2684
* 9 7 8 1 9 5 3 2 8 5 7 7 5 *